MEET FRANKIE JORDAN by Kim C. Lee
Illustrated by Vera Sysolina
Published by Kim C. Lee

Copyright © 2020 Kim C. Lee.

All rights reserved. No part of this publication may be reproduced, distributed, or transmitted in any form or by any means —electronic, mechanical, photocopy, recording, or otherwise — without prior written permission of the publisher or author. For permission requests, contact the author at: info@kimcleewrites.com

ISBN: 978-1-7361273-0-8

Visit the author's website at www.kimcleewrites.com.

Meet Frankie Jordan

Written by
Kim C. Lee

Illustrated by
Vera Sysolina

for
Aaliyah & Alanah

This is my friend,
FRANKIE.

Frankie Jordan,
to be exact.

She spends
her free time doodling
as an illustrator –

THIS IS FACT!

Frankie sees the world in many COLORS, patterns and textures galore!

CREATIVITY is the superpower
that she will use to change the world!

Frankie is comfortable in sneakers and wears a soft and FUZZY scarf.

Her ringlets bounce from here to there
and her skin is never parched.

Frankie can
tell you about

**Kahlo,
Basquiat
and Dalí.**

She's super motivated
by the work
of Studio Ghibli.

The kids at school sometimes call her WEIRD.

They tease and they point,
they laugh, and they jeer.

They just don't get it –
ART is silly to them!
They ask Frankie to be
NORMAL,
normal just like them.

They ask her
to ride bikes
and jump rope
like they do.

They question her
lack of excitement
to play dress up
in costumes.

They want Frankie
to enjoy dodge ball,
play hide-and-seek
or tag.

Her schoolmates
are so normal
that they cannot
ZIG or ZAG!

I tell them Frankie is

DIFFERENT,

but perfectly herself!

Frankie has

NO INTEREST

in being someone else.

I am
INSPIRED
by her sneakers.
I love her soft
and fuzzy scarf!

I am impressed by
her commitment
and her focus on her
ART!

I like to watch her

CREATE

with a pencil
and sketching pad!

To practice
drawing daffodils
is good
and nothing bad.

She draws daffodils as she sees them.
She draws daffodils with arms and legs!

She draws them at the dining room table cracking breakfast eggs!

Frankie imagines the

TICKLE MONSTER

as a blue polka-dotted creature.

She draws him smiling with golden horns saying,

"HI, IT'S NICE TO MEET YA!"

Frankie is

INNOVATIVE

and has a huge

IMAGINATION.

There is nothing that she can't do
when drawing an illustration.

What Frankie does
may seem weird
if you like to do other things,
but Frankie's

HEART

is dedicated to art,
it's as simple as coloring.

CREATIVITY

is her superpower
and she will use it to

CHANGE THE WORLD!

Frankie Jordan,
illustrator,
is quite an

AMAZING GIRL!

Do you know
someone like Frankie?
Someone that is
happy
JUST TO BE?

Someone

HAPPY

being the best version
of themselves
that they can be?

Maybe that person is YOU.
Do you do things unlike anyone else?

Have you ever liked something DIFFERENT, something different from everyone else?

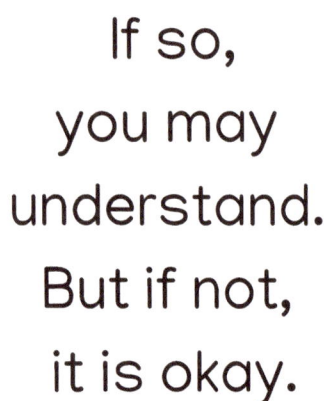

If so,
you may
understand.
But if not,
it is okay.

Most important
is that we agree
to accept all

UNIQUE

and

WONDERFUL

ways.

About the Author

Kim C. Lee is a children's book author from Maryland. Her writing is inspired by things in life that tickle the heart and she is especially motivated to create stories that resonate with her son and other children of diverse backgrounds. When she is not focused on finding the right words for a story, Kim enjoys spending time with family and friends, discovering new technologies, and dabbling in graphic design. Kim is a member of the Society of Children's Book Writers and Illustrators. Find Kim online at www.kimcleewrites.com.

In July 2020, Kim published her first children's book, The Night Owl. In this story, readers follow the post-bedtime adventures of the Night Owl, a young boy determined not to fall asleep. Based on personal experiences with an occasional sleep adverse child, this tale is undoubtedly relatable to all ages and guaranteed to leave readers heading to bed with a smile!

Famous Faces in Art

ZORA NEAL HURSTON
Author, filmmaker and anthropologist

SALVADOR DALÍ
Author, photographer, painter, illustrator

AARON DOUGLAS
Painter and graphic artist

JEAN-MICHEL BASQUIAT
Poet, musician, and graffiti artist

FRIDA KAHLO
Painter

CPSIA information can be obtained
at www.ICGtesting.com
Printed in the USA
JSHW072118160223
37833JS00001B/1